D1527795

OTHER BOOKS BY JOSEPH ....

full-length:

Areas of Fog (Shearsman, 2009)
At the Point (Shearsman, 2011)
To Keep Time (Omnidawn, 2014)
Illocality (Wave, 2015)
A New Silence (Shearsman, 2019)
Rosary Made of Air (The Exile Press, 2022)

chapbooks:

Minima St. (Range, 2003)
Eureka Slough (Effing Press, 2005)
Bramble (Hot Whiskey, 2005)
Property Line (Fewer & Further, 2006)
November Graph (Longhouse, 2007)
Out of Light (Kitchen Press, 2008)
Within Hours (Fault Line Press, 2008)
The Lack Of (Nasturtium Press, 2009)
Exit North (Book Thug, 2010)
Mock Orange (Longhouse, 2010)
Another Rehearsal for Morning (Longhouse, 2011)
Thaw Compass (Press Board Press, 2014)
An Interim (Tungsten Press, 2014)
What Follows (Ornithopter Press, 2015)
5 Poems (Tungsten Press, 2018)
Present Conditions (Hollyridge Press, 2018)
Backroad Scroll (Longhouse, 2019)
Unsent (Wrack Line Editions, 2019)

No Omen (Otata's Bookshelf, 2019)
On the Cusp (Tungsten Press, 2021)
Breath Work (The Exile Press, 2022)

THE LIGHT *of* NO OTHER HOUR

Joseph Massey

THE EXILE PRESS 2023

Joseph Massey, The Light of No Other Hour
First published in 2023 by The Exile Press

ISBN: 9798392590834
Cover design and interior: Dan Rattelle, St
Brigid's Guild

Cover Photograph ©Joseph Massey

CONTENTS

for my Father

"And all is always now."

-T.S. Eliot

The poet has two jobs: write and survive. Between the two some kind of life occurs, close to the ground, in poverty. And there are seasons. Even as a snow squall pixelates the alley outside my window in the middle of May.

Poetry is time chiseled into a shape that makes a sound.

SOMA

I spent spring half-tethered
to a body that was and wasn't
mine. The form was familiar, but I
dangled beyond it. Was it
the mind, the thing that buzzed—
a sound straining to become
language, caught between blades of light
outshining a flowering pear tree.
I'm whole in summer's monotone;
I'm flesh in this heat.
I think through this body,
alive on a Friday, on a bench,
watching a wasp dodge traffic.
A wasp dissolving into chalk-white sun.

INTERCESSION

What's real
remains blurred
until we say
its name. Lord,
keep me tethered.
Grief burns
in my throat, but
morning slants
into a new season.
Pear trees
flower along
both sides of
the street
and flex
with wind,
off-white
and pixelated
like lungs
breathing memory
or a frame
from a dream
dissolving
before a shock of
forsythia spikes
the landscape yellow.
The colors flood
through me,
what's left of me

in the sudden
absence of thought.
Call it happiness.
Call it the center
of a prayer.
What's left of me
when the images
pour in
like a chant
or a charm
and scatter
into the seamless.
To see
by means
of the unseen.
Lord, keep me
tethered
to meaning:
Your silence
where all things
are holy.
All things
vibrating with
light, April
light. Light
with no winter
left in it. Light
of no other hour.

Spear Thistle

The heat seals
the day beneath
a sheet of faded sepia.

Summer is bardo—
gnat-flecked and feral.

Still, I covet wakefulness
in this season of sleep and the odd wildflower.

THE ROOM *is* SUMMER'S CHANNEL

i.

Evening opens song
expanding
into soundless dark.
That we're here—
that we're here at all
in summer's
gutter, moved to speak.

ii.

Thunderstorms gather,
dim the room,
indent the window
where sky sieves
gray through old glass; gray
now blue at
the brink of all black.

iii.

Even the shadows
swelter, webbed
across asphalt, fall-
en from tall
dandelions—a
heatwave's re-
lentless impressions.

iv.

Phantom pain in place
of human
touch. The room isn't
as quiet
as an other would
be. Make do
with night, reaching through.

v.

Lost in the mind, or
lost in the
world, I watch a storm
rake over
the mountain; fine lines
the wind slants
sideways, slurring sun.

vi.

How morning expands
the window
beyond itself, as
if the glass
were light and the frame
a thing blown
into the margins.

SUMMER WINDOW
for Asha Nayaswami

In the middle of the day,
light pulls away from the room
            like water at low tide
as black clouds crouch along the horizon.
            Black clouds framed by a window
that reminds me I'm alive
            when I wake up still stuck in dreaming.
Summer window, my source of vision
            in this impossible season.
The faint thunder's less faint now—
            overhead and driving
a spike through the top of my skull;
            and the mind, for a moment, forgets itself.
Blurred behind a lamp's amber reflection,
            I watch rain fall
and lightning—the flash repeating
            as an echo in my inner-eye.

the blur
between
blue and green

the mountain
smothered

in summer's
color

CLOSER *to* OCTOBER

Potholes full of rings
of rain ex-
panding, vanishing

into each other.
Gone, lost in
these infinities,

I walk the seam where
summer with-
draws. Cold rain devoid

of even a trace
of August.
Rust on the maples

and on the Kousa
dogwoods: red
berries beaming through

the gathering gloom.

FAR

Your silence
is as full
as anything spoken

or sung,
or found far
in October-deep

limbs
patterned
around a pond

I thought was a lake
for the landscape
of color reflected—

the crowded
maples, embers
in waves.

LATE OCTOBER

To walk through this light
is to cross a threshold that
has no obvious
end, but night drapes the landscape
before you've had time to think.

COMPANY

The shadow
of my body
filled in
with red leaves.

*

Stand in the center—
the mirror
the puddle becomes.

*

Starlings billow low
then high, one mind

shifting shape
in purple dusk.

DEEP NOVEMBER

Fog droops
over a narrow creek.

Limbs shook bare
claw their reflection

into brackish water
lapping a retainer wall

stained with blue graffiti.
What the heart can't hold

the mind churns into static
the day alone decodes.

But the wind—
the first syllable of winter—

needles my face numb
and my hands, numb,

raise up an absence.

AFTER *a* LONG DEPRESSION

The distortion lifts
and the mind,
organized, finds
the signal
the season sends in
clear gray waves
rough leaves billow through.

shaken by the scent
of honeysuckle, I slip
from present to past

DEAR CID

What you left
behind, this
sheaf of language

breathing—
in the wordless night
you're alive

in mind. My heart
pinched, pinned
to a syllable.

Found Poem

for Jacqueline, in memory

i.

When we visited
Dickinson's grave our
shadows crossed the stone—
crossed out "CALLED
BACK." What else was there
to say or to see.

ii.

This is translation,
this is poetry,
the alchemy in
        a word—in
death—you continue
        to pronounce yourself.

iii.

    I imagine you
wanted, finally,
to be free from words—
        in the rain
ghost-pale petals drift
      beyond metaphor.

iv.

    The space between lines—
horizon on top
of horizon, where
      you wait for
meaning to rise from
    silence—a small sun.

v.

Fat bees vault between
blossoms, loop through light
the wind can't contain—
       winter gone
in colors flooding
      the margin of you.

vi.

    Nameless, wordless light,
this is what remains
of you: the outline
       of a dream
drawn deeper into
     dawn—into morning.

vii.

    And now you're nowhere
being everywhere
at once, found and un-
        found, without
language to brace you
      from becoming earth.

FOR NOW

Blocks away a siren aligns
with the whine of a bird

I can't identify
in unobstructed sun.

The world is what reaches

through the weather
we're under. How
the day suddenly

escapes memory.
Here and there,
equally speechless.

Before Mass

After a night
wracked with panic,

it's a gift to sit
in the center
of a motionless hour.

Stained-glass
glazing vacant pews.

PILGRIM

{on the Feast Day of St. Benedict Joseph Labre}

Emptied of the world,
you walked the earth

(God-gone
and God-given)

in an undertow
of prayer.

In a crown of gnats
you swooned

and slept.
Saint,

on your feast day
when the rain passed

a dozen potholes
held a dozen suns.

SAINT BRIGID'S

Gravestones, nameless
after a century of weather—

shadows stream
narrow-limbed

over uneven ground.
Summer's first murmur:

gnats and honeysuckle
cloud the cemetery's

night-green edge—
green throbbing

and slowly tumbling in.
I sit

with the stones
until silence

abides silence.
Mercy.

How we're all always turning
back into earth.

PRAYER WALK

At summer's brink,
yellow forsythia haze
dissipates into thunder

and petrichor. Spring
was a memory
of spring.

Bone-thin trees
drift from their roots
in a ditch filled with dark weeds.

Peepers quaver
and go on quavering—
the sound the mind makes

when panic
seizes thought.
But tonight the mind is still,

cinched to silence
by syllables
vibrating through

a loop of beads.

a broken line of
geese rowing
silently through snow

BEADS

i.

A dream
disintegrates
into a room—

my body
made of
light.

ii.

I don't notice
until I'm surrounded,

my senses seized
by the season.

Leaf-tides
sidewind
asphalt;

color clots
sewer grates.

iii.

The flare
and the fire
bright before
dying—

November's
quick
turn
inward

turns
the mind
inside-out.

iv.

Freezing air
cuts through
closed windows,
encapsulating pain.

The poem glows
unwritten
in the center of
the room.

v.

An inner-silence
blots out nostalgia.

What was left
unspent
in autumn
withers
under ice.

Now the new life;
the holy order

of dawn breaking.

vi.

First, the maples turn.
Embers fill the field.

The maples turn
before the mind turns

to face the season.
What would it mean

for October
to think through me?

Give myself over
to the rhythm

of things decaying?
These beads of wordless prayer

reeling in
the early dark.

The Last Poem

It is enough
to be nothing,
porous
to what appears.
It is enough

to sit on a bench
and watch a contrail
dissolve into dust,
to make a day of it.

It is enough
to look
in order to see,
and to know
there's a difference.

It is enough
to walk myself awake
in sub-zero wind,

snow-blind
and heartbroken.
It is enough
to forget.

It is enough
to borrow
from the dead
a voice

to sing through,
to survive the season.

It is enough,
the poems cramped
in the margins
of a water-stained
notebook——

leave them there
to be revised
by time.

It is enough——

alone
at the end of the year
engulfed by a presence
I am not compelled to name.

Lux Brumalis

i.

Lately, poetry
and prayer
reconcile silence.

Collapsing
into dawn, you see
how night lacked
nothing—darkness spoke.

ii.

Abbreviated
days engrave
shadow into stone.

iii.

Red winter sunset—
even the pavement

in this vacant parking lot
softens under the color.

iv.

Windblown snow in sun—
a friend's voice
dissolving the ache.

v.

Gnarled limbs
grapple air—
air made visible

through undone
columns of snow.

vi.

The inaudible
syllable—
half moon in daylight.

vii.

Brittle syllables,
bitter prayer,

and freezing air
held in my palms.

viii.

Over thinning snow
shadows of
dead flowers flail.

THREE MORNINGS *in* MARCH

i.

At the seam
between sleep
and consciousness,
morning birds
and rain
mirror
the shape
of the room.

ii.

Through a snow squall, I
walked home and knew Your presence
in the visibly
invisible, and the sting
when the wind changed direction.

iii.

Here in the dying
world, in God's
sleep, geese
lift up

       and out
of the half-thawed pond.

LENTEN SYLLABLES

i.

This false spring, this un-
raveling sorrow, O God,
and these sparrows in
a mangled shrub, how they form
a body—head gone in song.

ii.

After a false spring
when the sun returns to dust
and the clouds are dust,
the geese—pulled into a point—
puncture dull and blinding gray.

iii.

Gone white overnight,
the mountain presses into
hovering gray sky.
Geese in the shape of a snapped
arrow——chant echoing chant.

iv.

As the ashen snow
melts, gutters become dream-blurred
mirrors reflecting
wire-thin branches scrawled across
traffic and a dying sun.

v. (Coda)

A voice in the night   the sound of snow
falling through snow   a voice thin with prayer
and winter   and a memory of light
perforated by spring   the sound of snow
whirling around streetlights   an imagined sound
honed by the cold and held in mind   a voice
in the night that needs no response
beyond acknowledgment   the listening
this leaning in to decipher precisely nothing.

UNSEASONABLY

i.

Spring coming in now, in the light, in these
scintillated edges when it touches a thing, and
returns things – say, the dormant globe
thistle, rows of faded gravestones, the ragged
sparrow perched on a chain-link fence – to
their names. We catch our breath and wait.
Tomorrow, snow.

ii.

The delirium of spring: colors emerging, margins blurred. Wind spinning bright shackles over the pond before dispersing into a warped reflection of the sky. In this weather, I walk a half-step beyond my body. In this weather, I practice death. Pale, carbonated light, within which all things from a distance appear to levitate.

iii.

April's unrecognizable. Each breeze a husk of
summer's bloodlessness. Insects the size of a
fist. No, the heart can't catch up, torn into
sepia grief. Every wild and nameless thing
mindlessly reaching. I look for you in the blur
— a face to anchor my mind in the real.

iv.

Some color returns. Incandescent green
horizon. Listen to frogs trill deep in the brush
and know it is spring. A flowering pear tree
flickers white through a torn curtain of rain. A
swallow cuts against the current and vanishes.
This is the sacrament of the present moment.
Time passes through the body, leaving a poem
in the mouth.

To listen, and to wait. To find a phrase to tamp down terror, a sentence to absorb the dread. To extract from the abstract a fragrance of the real. To break the line at the apex of a breath. To follow the breath. To watch swallows swell in unison from a sagging power line and fan out across a sky mottled with clouds — a dissolving syntax of clouds. To notice, and to go on noticing. To say so. There is no other task.

Joseph Massey is the author of *Rosary Made of Air* (The Exile Press, 2022), *A New Silence* (Shearsman Books, 2019), *Illocality* (Wave Books, 2015), and a trilogy grounded in the landscape of coastal Humboldt County, California: *Areas of Fog* (Shearsman Books, 2009), *At the Point* (Shearsman Books, 2011), and *To Keep Time* (Omnidawn, 2014).

His work has appeared in many journals and magazines, including *The Nation, A Public Space, American Poet: The Journal of the Academy of American Poets, Verse, GeoHumanities, Talisman,* and in anthologies: *Visiting Dr. Williams: Poems Inspired by the Life and Work of William Carlos Williams* (University of Iowa Press, 2011), *Haiku in English: The First Hundred Years* (W.W. Norton & Company, 2013), *Please Excuse This Poem: 100 New Poems for the Next Generation* (Viking Penguin, 2015), and *The Poem Is You: 60 Contemporary American Poems and How to Read Them* (Belknap Press, 2016).

His poems have been translated into French, Dutch, Bengali, Finnish, Czech, and Portuguese.

Made in the USA
Monee, IL
07 June 2023

35395490R00049